Learn to Make Sushi

with The Simplest

Cookbook

20+ Sushi Recipes with Simple Instructions for

Beginners

BY

MOLLY MILLS

License Notes

No part of this book may be copied, replicated, distributed, sold or shared without the express and written consent of the Author.

The ideas expressed in the book are for entertainment purposes. The Reader assumes all risk when following any guidelines and the Author accepts no responsibility if damages occur due to actions taken by the Reader.

An Amazing Offer for Buying My Book!

Thank you very much for purchasing my books! As a token of my appreciation, I would like to extend an amazing offer to you! When you have subscribed with your e-mail address, you will have the opportunity to get free and discounted e-books that will show up in your inbox daily. You will also receive reminders before an offer expires so you never miss out. With just little effort on your part, you will have access to the newest and most informative books at your fingertips. This is all part of the VIP treatment when you subscribe below.

SIGN ME UP: *https://molly.gr8.com*

Table of Contents

Chapter I - The Benefits of Eating Sushi

It is no secret that sushi is considered to be a pretty healthy food source, especially where it originally originates from. Sushi itself is packed full of fresh fish which is high in healthy antioxidants and omega fatty acids and healthy vegetables that are filled with fiber and beneficial nutrients that your body naturally craves for.

In this chapter you will learn about all of the benefits sushi holds for you and how it can help to improve your health in the long run.

AAAAAAAAAAAAAAAAAAAAAAAAAAAAAAAAAAAAAAAAA

(1) Sushi Is Packed Full of Nutrients

The one thing that people don't realize is that the outer wrap of most types of sushi, the seaweed wrap, is considered an important food staple in Japanese cuisine today. This small wrap is packed full of beneficial nutrients that your body craves such as Vitamins a and B6 as well as various minerals such as iodine.

Seaweed itself is also low in calories and packed full of protein, which can help lower risks of high blood pressure and has been proven to improve the health of your heart.

AAAAAAAAAAAAAAAAAAAAAAAAAAAAAAAAAAAAAAAAA

(2) Low in Calories

Many traditional sushi rolls are often made by combining different types of raw fish, different vegetables, steamed rice and wraps of seaweed and wrapping them together in small bundles for you to enjoy. What many people don't realize is that these pieces of sushi are low in calories.

Let's look at some examples. A classic salmon roll that is wrapped in seaweed and contains a bit of cucumber only contains about 231 calories and only 4 grams of fat. A roll of shrimp contains about 200 calories and contains 0 grams of fat.

If that is just too many calories for you, you can easily cut your calories in half by leaving out some ingredients. For example you can remove the raw fish and instead pack your sushi with vegetables instead or just enjoy a piece of sashimi. Remember, if you are trying to watch your calories, remove some food products such as tempura or any type of spicy sauce as these will have more calories than anything.

Either way you can rest assured that you are getting a low calorie meal without the added fat in the process.

AAAAAAAAAAAAAAAAAAAAAAAAAAAAAAAAAAAAAAAA

(3) Packed Full of Vegetables

In order to gain the most benefits out of consuming sushi as often as possible, the best way to do so is to fill your sushi with delicious and nutritious vegetables and condiments. For example, if you are making a California roll, the best way to make it healthy is to add a touch of avocado which is considered to be a healthy fat source for you. If you need to increase your intake of fiber, then I highly recommend making sushi with healthy brown rice instead of steamed white rice.

And don't forget to include some tasty condiments with your meal! For example serve your sushi with some wasabi which is high in helpful antioxidants or some ginger which can help to alleviate any stomach issue as well as work as an antimicrobial agents.

(4) Beneficial Fish

Most of the health benefits of sushi come from the fish that is packed inside. I am sure that most of you are aware that fish itself is rich in protein and Omega 3 and 6 fatty acids which has been proven to help give your hair a naturally shiny appearance, help to improve your eyesight and can help reduce the chance of developing heart conditions. Fish is also rich in a mineral known as Selenium. This mineral has been proven to help protect those against the development of cancer.

Remember, sushi itself does not have to contain fish in order for it to be beneficial. You can fill it with other fillings such as eel, shrimp or even scallops. It will still be beneficial and incredibly delicious.

AAAAAAAAAAAAAAAAAAAAAAAAAAAAAAAAAAAAAAAAAA

Chapter II - Tips for Making Sushi at Home

At first glance it may seem that making sushi from your home is quite difficult. However, the more you practice, the easier it will become. When you first try your hand at making sushi for yourself, there are a few things that you will want to keep in mind as you do so, so you can make the most delicious sushi you have ever tasted.

In this chapter you will learn various tips and tricks to making the best sushi ever and to make the entire sushi making process easier on yourself.

AAAAAAAAAAAAAAAAAAAAAAAAAAAAAAAAAAAAAAAA

(1) Take It Easy

There is no point in stressing yourself over making sushi. So my first tip to you is to just take it easy and relax. Making sushi takes a large and often times difficult learning curve. It takes time, patience and plenty of practice to make the perfect sushi each and every time. So, there is no need for you to unnecessarily stress yourself over it in the process.

Keep in mind that your first attempts at making sushi may end up just being one huge mess. Either way it will taste amazing so just relax.

AAAAAAAAAAAAAAAAAAAAAAAAAAAAAAAAAAAAAAAAA

(2) Always Use the Sharpest of Knives

I know that this may sound like dumb advice, but you will thank me for it later. When you cut sushi you only want to use the sharpest of knives in order to do so. I also recommend wetting your knives slightly before you cut your sushi as this will help to prevent your sushi roll from tearing as you cut.

AAAAAAAAAAAAAAAAAAAAAAAAAAAAAAAAAAAAAAAAA

(3) Don't Overstuff Your Sushi

I know that when you first begin making sushi, how tempting it can be to pack it full of every ingredient and filling that you want to use. I am here to caution you against these for many reasons. If you try to overstuff your sushi, the only thing that may happen is that your sushi won't roll up properly, your ingredients could end up becoming squished, your sushi roll can end up popping open or all of your fillings will come out on the sides.

The best thing that you can do instead is just to fill it to the bare minimum and take it as is. Either way your sushi will look beautiful as well taste amazing.

AAAAAAAAAAAAAAAAAAAAAAAAAAAAAAAAAAAAAAAA

(4) Watch Out for Sticky Rice

While steamed Japanese style rice is undoubtedly delicious, however it has been known to make quite the mess out of everything. The bad part about this type of rice is that it can stick to everything and anything. So, when using this type of rice, always wash your hands after handling it so you can avoid tracking it everywhere around your home.

AAAAAAAAAAAAAAAAAAAAAAAAAAAAAAAAAAAAAAAAA

(5) Use the Lightest of Pressure to Roll Your Sushi

When you are using a bamboo mat to roll your sushi, remember that you do not need to use a ton of pressure in order to keep your sushi together as you roll it. The gentlest of pressures will do just fine. If you use too much pressure, you can risk your roll of sushi coming out as an odd shape or can cause it not to stick together at all.

AAAAAAAAAAAAAAAAAAAAAAAAAAAAAAAAAAAAAAAAAA

Chapter III - Tasty Sushi Recipes

AAAAAAAAAAAAAAAAAAAAAAAAAAAAAAAAAAAAAAAA

Recipe 1: Shrimp Packed Sushi

If you are a huge fan of shrimp, then you need to try this shrimp sushi dish out for yourself. It is extremely tender and great when served with some soy sauce. This is certainly a sushi dish that any sushi enthusiast will fall in love.

Yield: 8 Servings

Cooking Time: 25 Minutes

List of Ingredients:

- 10 Pieces of Shrimp, Uncooked
- 1 Cup of Water
- 2 Tablespoons of Vinegar, Rice Variety
- 2 Bowls of Rice, White and Sushi Variety
- 2 Tablespoons of Wasabi
- Some Soy Sauce, For Dipping

AAAAAAAAAAAAAAAAAAAAAAAAAAAAAAAAAAAAAAA

Instructions:

1. The first thing that you will want to do is cook up your shrimp. To do this heat up your water over medium to high heat until it begins to boil. Once boiling add in your shrimp and allow to cook for the next 3 to 5 minutes. Remove and dip into ice water to stop the cooking process.

2. Once chilled remove the shell from your shrimp. Cut and prepare your shrimp as you normally would.

3. Then mix together your vinegar with your rice, making sure to stir thoroughly until evenly mixed together.

4. Next place your seaweed onto a bamboo mat. Then place a thin layer of rice onto your seaweed.

5. Add your remaining ingredients on top of your rice and spread evenly throughout your rice. Press down lightly to press into the rice.

6. Wet the edges of your seaweed and begin to roll your sushi from the bottom tightly. Once rolled cut your roll into 8 equal sized pieces and repeat as necessary. Serve with some of your favorite soy sauce and strips of ginger and enjoy.

Recipe 2: Classic California Roll

This is a simple sushi recipe that happens to be a fan favorite of many people out there. It is incredibly delicious and simple to make. Once you get a bite of this dish you won't be able to stop at just one.

Yield: 8 Servings

Cooking Time: 1 Hour and 30 Minutes

List of Ingredients:

- 1 Cup of Rice, Uncooked and Sushi Variety
- 1 Cup of Water
- ¼ Cup of Vinegar, Rice Style
- 1 tablespoon of Sugar, White
- ½ Cup of Crabmeat, Imitation Variety and Chopped Finely
- ¼ Cup of Mayonnaise
- 8 Sheets of Seaweed, Dry
- 2 ½ Tablespoons of Sesame Seeds
- 1 Cucumber, Fresh and Cut Into Thin Pieces
- 2 Avocados, Peeled and Sliced Into Thin Pieces

AAAAAAAAAAAAAAAAAAAAAAAAAAAAAAAAAAAAAAAA

Instructions:

1. The first thing that you will want to do is cook your rice. To do this bring both your rice and water together in a medium sized saucepan. Heat over high heat and once boiling reduce the heat to a simmer and allow your rice to cook until it is tender and the liquid has been fully absorbed. This should take about 20 minutes.

2. Then stir together your rice style vinegar and white sugar together in a small sized bowl until your sugar full dissolves. Stir this mixture into your rice until thoroughly mixed together. Allow your rice to cool completely and then set aside for later use.

3. Next combine your crabmeat and mayo together in a small sized bowl, stirring thoroughly until evenly combined.

4. Next place your seaweed onto a bamboo mat. Then place a thin layer of rice onto your seaweed.

5. Add your remaining ingredients on top of your rice and spread evenly throughout your rice. Press down lightly to press into the rice.

6. Wet the edges of your seaweed and begin to roll your sushi from the bottom tightly. Once rolled cut your roll into 5 to 6 equal sized pieces and repeat as necessary. Serve with some of your favorite soy sauce and strips of ginger and enjoy.

Recipe 3: Spicy Tuna Sushi

This is a great tasting sushi dish with a bit of a kick behind it. For the tastiest results cook your tuna according to your own preference so you can bring out the most delicious flavors in your dish.

Yield: 4 Servings

Cooking Time: 1 Hour and 45 Minutes

List of Ingredients:

- 2 Cups of Rice, White and Sushi Variety
- 2 ½ Cups of Water
- 1 tablespoon of Vinegar, Rice Variety
- 1 Can of Tuna, In Water and Drained
- 1 tablespoon of Mayonnaise
- 1 teaspoon of Chili Powder
- 1 teaspoon of Wasabi
- 4 Seaweed Sheets, Dry
- ½ a Cucumber, Diced Finely
- 1 Avocado, Peeled and Finely Diced

AAAAAAAAAAAAAAAAAAAAAAAAAAAAAAAAAAAAAAAA

Instructions:

1. The first thing that you will want to do is cook your rice. To do this bring your rice, rice vinegar and water together in a medium sized saucepan. Heat over high heat and once boiling reduce the heat to a simmer and allow your rice to cook until it is tender and the liquid has been fully absorbed. This should take about 20 minutes.

2. Then stir together your canned tuna, mayo wasabi and chili powder in a small sized bowl until your sugar full dissolves. Stir this mixture thoroughly until your tuna begins to break apart easily. Make sure your mixture does not form a paste.

3. Next place your seaweed onto a bamboo mat. Then place a thin layer of rice onto your seaweed.

4. Add your remaining ingredients on top of your rice and spread evenly throughout your rice. Press down lightly to press into the rice.

5. Wet the edges of your seaweed and begin to roll your sushi from the bottom tightly. Once rolled cut your roll into 6 to 8 equal sized pieces and repeat as necessary. Serve with some of your favorite soy sauce and strips of ginger and enjoy.

Recipe 4: Easy Smoked Salmon Sushi

This is the perfect sushi recipe to begin with if you are a beginner. It is my personal favorite type of sushi and I know once you try it, it will become yours too.

Yield: 6 Servings

Cooking Time: 5 Hours

List of Ingredients:

- 2 Cups of Rice, Japanese Style and Sushi Variety
- 6 Tablespoons of Vinegar, Rice Wine Variety
- 6 Sheets of Seaweed, Dry
- 1 Avocado, Peeled and Finely Sliced
- 1 Cucumber, Peeled and Finely Sliced
- 8 Ounces of Salmon, Smoked and Cut Into thin Strips
- 2 Tablespoons of Wasabi

AAAAAAAAAAAAAAAAAAAAAAAAAAAAAAAAAAAAAAAA

Instructions:

1. The first thing that you will want to do is soak your Japanese rice for at least 4 hours. After this time drain your rice and add into a rice cooker with at least 2 cups of water.

2. Once your rice is cooked mix in your vinegar and stir to evenly coat your rice. Next spread your rice out on a plate to cool completely.

3. Next place 1 sheet of your seaweed onto a bamboo mat. Then place a thin layer of rice onto your seaweed, making sure to leave some of the seaweed at the top uncovered.

4. Dot small amounts of your wasabi on top of your rice and add your remaining ingredients evenly on top.

5. Wet the edges of your seaweed and begin to roll your sushi from the bottom tightly. Once rolled cut your roll into 8 equal sized pieces and repeat as necessary. Serve with some of your favorite soy sauce and strips of ginger and enjoy.

Recipe 5: Hot Scallop Sushi

If you are a fan of scallops, then this is the perfect dish for you. This is a tasty and spicy sushi recipe that I know you are just going to love.

Yield: 8 Servings

Cooking Time: 20 Minutes

List of Ingredients:

- ¾ Cup of Rice, Sushi Variety
- 1 Sheet of Seaweed, Dry
- 4 Scallops, Fresh and Diced
- 2 Tablespoons of Peanuts, Coarse and Crushed
- 2 Tablespoons of Mayo, Japanese Style
- Dash of Chili Pepper Flakes, For Taste
- 1 Carrot, Fresh, Steamed and Diced Finely

AAAAAAAAAAAAAAAAAAAAAAAAAAAAAAAAAAAAAAAA

Instructions:

1. The first thing that you will want to do is take out a large sized pan and add in your oil. Heat over medium and add in your scallops. Sear until light gold in color and remove from heat.

2. Mix your remaining ingredients together with your seared scallops in a medium sized bowl, making sure to stir thoroughly until evenly mixed together.

3. Next place your seaweed onto a bamboo mat. Then place a thin layer of rice onto your seaweed.

4. Add your remaining ingredients on top of your rice and spread evenly throughout your rice. Press down lightly to press into the rice.

5. Wet the edges of your seaweed and begin to roll your sushi from the bottom tightly. Once rolled cut your roll into 6 pieces and repeat as necessary. Serve with some of your favorite soy sauce and strips of ginger and enjoy.

Recipe 6: Southern Style Sushi

This is a wholesome lunch or dinner dish that you can make when you are craving something a little more wholesome. I know you are just going to love it.

Yield: 6 Servings

Cooking Time: 25 Minutes

List of Ingredients:

- 1 ¼ Cups of Rice, Sushi Variety and White in Color
- ¼ Cup of Cream Sauce, Gorgonzola Variety
- 2 Tablespoons of Gorgonzola, Crumbled
- 4 Stalks of Asparagus, Grilled and Cut Into Thin Strips
- 6 Ounces of Flank Steak, Grilled and Cut into Thin Strips
- Dash of Salt For Taste
- Dash of Pepper For Taste

AAAAAAAAAAAAAAAAAAAAAAAAAAAAAAAAAAAAAAAAAA

Instructions:

1. Use a large sized bowl and combine your first 3 ingredients together and stir together until your rice is fully coated.

2. Roll your rice mixture into small sized bowl until you make at least 12 pieces of rice.

3. Top each piece of sushi with your flank steak and wrap around your rice roll completely.

4. Season your sushi with a dash of salt and pepper and serve with some extra cream serve for the tastiest results. Enjoy!

Recipe 7: Classic Sushi Roll

When you make sushi, you can fill it with whatever kind of ingredients you like. You can try salmon, crab meat or even lobster. For the tastiest results serve this sushi with some wasabi and soy sauce.

Yield: 8 Servings

Cooking Time: 45 Minutes

List of Ingredients:

- 2/3 Cup of White Rice, Uncooked and Short Grain Variety
- 3 Tablespoons of Vinegar, Rice Variety
- 3 Tablespoons of Sugar, White
- 1 ½ teaspoons of Salt
- 4 Sheets of Seaweed
- ½ of a Cucumber, Peeled and Cut into Thin Strips
- 2 Tablespoons of Ginger, Pickled
- 1 Avocado, Peeled
- ½ Pound of Crabmeat, Imitation Variety and Flaked

AAAAAAAAAAAAAAAAAAAAAAAAAAAAAAAAAAAAAAAAAA

Instructions:

1. The first thing that you will want to do is soak your Japanese rice for at least 4 hours. After this time drain your rice and add into a rice cooker with your water.

2. Once your rice is cooked mix in your vinegar and stir to evenly coat your rice. Then add in your sugar, vinegar and salt and stir to thoroughly combine. Next spread your rice out on a plate to cool completely.

3. Next place 1 sheet of your seaweed onto a bamboo mat. Then place a thin layer of rice onto your seaweed.

4. Add your remaining ingredients on top of your rice and spread evenly throughout your rice. Press down lightly to press into the rice.

5. Wet the edges of your seaweed and begin to roll your sushi from the bottom tightly. Once rolled cut your roll into 6 to 8 equal sized pieces and repeat as necessary. Serve with some of your favorite soy sauce and strips of ginger and enjoy.

Recipe 8: Breakfast Style Sushi

If you are looking for a way to change up your breakfast menu, then there is no better way to do so then with this sushi dish. These rolls contain delicious breakfast items such as cream cheese and eggs, making for a tasty sushi dish that you won't be able to get enough of.

Yield: 8 Servings

Cooking Time: 25 Minutes

List of Ingredients:

- 2 Sheets of Seaweed, Dry
- ¾ Pound of Salmon, Smoked Varity and Cut into Thin Strips
- ½ Cup of Onion, Green in Color and Minced
- 1 Bell Pepper, Green in Color and Cut Julienne Style
- 1 Ounce of Cream Cheese, Soft
- 2 Eggs, Large in Size and Beaten
- 1 Egg, Yolk Only
- 2 Tablespoons of Butter, Soft
- ¼ Cup of Milk, Whole
- 1 teaspoon of Lemon, Juice Only
- ¼ Cup of Water
- 2 Ounces of Soy Sauce, Sweet Variety
- ¼ Ounce of Ginger, Crystalized Variety

AAAAAAAAAAAAAAAAAAAAAAAAAAAAAAAAAAAAAAAA

Instructions:

1. First cook up your eggs. To do this preheat a medium sized skillet set over medium heat. While your skillet is heating up, crack your egg into a small sized bowl and whisk together with a dash of salt, making sure to whisk thoroughly to combine.

2. Pour your eggs into your hot skillet and cook until thoroughly scrambled and fully set.

3. Next place your seaweed onto a bamboo mat. Place your cooked egg onto your dry seaweed sheet. The top with your cream cheese, smoked salmon, pepper and onions.

4. Wet the edges of your seaweed and begin to roll your sushi from the bottom tightly. Once rolled cut your roll into 8 equal sized pieces and repeat as necessary. Serve with some of your favorite soy sauce and strips of ginger and enjoy.

5. Next mix together your remaining ingredients together in a medium sized saucepan and place over medium heat. Bring this mixture to a light simmer and cook until your sauce thickens up. Once thick in consistency reduce your heat and stir in your fresh lemon juice. Stir again and drizzle mixture over your rolled sushi.

Recipe 9: Mackerel Oshi Sushi

This is perhaps one of the oldest types of sushi you will ever make. This particular sushi recipe was made popular over 50 years ago and it is the primary reason as to why and how sushi dishes exists today. After one bite I know you won't be able to get enough of it.

Yield: 2 Servings

Cooking Time: 10 Minutes

List of Ingredients:

- 1 Mackerel, Horse Variety
- Dash of Salt for Taste
- Some Ginger, Finely Sliced
- 5 Leaves of Seaweed, Dry
- 1 Cup of Premade Rice, Sushi Variety

AAAAAAAAAAAAAAAAAAAAAAAAAAAAAAAAAAAAAAAAAAA

Instructions:

1. Next place 1 sheet of your seaweed onto a bamboo mat. Then place a thin layer of rice onto your seaweed, making sure to leave some of the seaweed at the top uncovered.

2. Dice up your mackerel finely into bite sized pieces and lay on top of your premade rice. Season with a dash of rice

3. Wet the edges of your seaweed and begin to roll your sushi from the bottom tightly. Once rolled cut your roll into 6 to 8 equal sized pieces and repeat as necessary. Serve with some of your favorite soy sauce and strips of ginger and enjoy.

Recipe 10: Delicious Temaki Salmon Sushi

Here is yet another salmon sushi dish that you are going to love. This particular salmon sushi dish is packed full of bold flavors that I know you won't be able to get enough of.

Yield: 8 Servings

Cooking Time: 15 Minutes

List of Ingredients:

- 1 Cup of Rice, Sushi Variety and Fully Cooked
- 2 Sheets of Seaweed, Dry
- 4 Pieces of Salmon, Sashimi Style and Cut Into Thin Strips
- 4 Leaves of Shiso
- 1 Cucumber, Peeled and Cut Into Thin Strips

AAAAAAAAAAAAAAAAAAAAAAAAAAAAAAAAAAAAAAAA

Instructions:

1. Next place your seaweed onto a bamboo mat. Then place a thin layer of rice onto your seaweed.

2. Add your remaining ingredients on top of your rice and spread evenly throughout your rice. Press down lightly to press into the rice.

3. Wet the edges of your seaweed and begin to roll your sushi from the bottom tightly. Once rolled cut your roll into 8 to 10 equal sized pieces and repeat as necessary. Serve with some of your favorite soy sauce and strips of ginger and enjoy.

Recipe 11: Tasty Avocado and Cucumber Sushi

This is the perfect sushi recipe to make if you are looking for something simple, yet delicious. Similar to nearly every type of sushi out there, feel free to add in whatever type of fish you want to this sushi.

Yield: 6 Servings

Cooking Time: 1 Hour

List of Ingredients:

- 1 ¼ Cups of Water
- 1 Cup of Rice, White and Sushi Variety
- 3 Tablespoons of Vinegar, Rice Variety
- Dash of Salt, For Taste
- 4 Sheets of Seaweed, Dry
- ½ Of A Cucumber, Sliced Into Strips
- 1 Avocado, Peeled and Finely Sliced

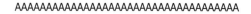

AAAAAAAAAAAAAAAAAAAAAAAAAAAAAAAAAAAAAAAA

Instructions:

1. The first thing that you will want to do is make your rice. To do this bring your water and rice together in a medium sized saucepan. Bring to a boil. Then cover, reduce the heat and allow your rice to cook for at least 20 minutes or until your rice is tender and the water is fully absorbed. Remove from heat and season with your dash of salt and your vinegar, stirring well to combine.

2. Next place 1 sheet of your seaweed onto a bamboo mat. Then place a thin layer of rice onto your seaweed, making sure to leave some of the seaweed at the top uncovered.

3. Add your slices of avocado and cucumber onto your rice, making sure to spread it evenly over the surface.

4. Wet the edges of your seaweed and begin to roll your sushi from the bottom tightly. Once rolled cut your roll into 5 to 6 equal sized pieces and repeat as necessary. Serve with some of your favorite soy sauce and strips of ginger and enjoy.

Recipe 12: Mediterranean Trout Sushi

If you are a huge fan of classic Mediterranean style dishes, then I know you are going to love this recipe. Packed full of those tasty Mediterranean flavors that you love, I know this is one sushi recipe you will want to make over and over again.

Yield: 6 Servings

Cooking Time: 20 Minutes

List of Ingredients:

- 6 Ounces of Trout, Smoked Variety and Fully Cooked
- 2 Pieces of Asparagus, BBQ style
- ½ Bell Pepper, Red in Color, Broiled and Cut into Thin Pieces
- 2 teaspoons of Soy Sauce, Low in Sodium
- ½ Cup of Lettuce, Romaine Variety and Cut into Thin Pieces
- 2 Sheets of Seaweed, Dry
- 1 Cup of Rice, Sushi Variety and Fully Cooked
- Some Wasabi Mixed with Lemon Juice, For Servings and Dipping

AAAAAAAAAAAAAAAAAAAAAAAAAAAAAAAAAAAAAAA

Instructions:

1. The first boil your lettuce in some hot water until slightly wilted. Remove and drizzle with your soy sauce

2. Next place your seaweed onto a bamboo mat. Then place a thin layer of rice onto your seaweed.

3. Layer your remaining ingredients on top of your rice and spread evenly throughout your rice. Press down lightly to press into the rice.

4. Wet the edges of your seaweed and begin to roll your sushi from the bottom tightly. Once rolled cut your roll into 6 pieces and repeat as necessary. Serve with some of your favorite soy sauce and strips of ginger and enjoy.

Recipe 13: Korean Style Sushi

This is a Korean style inspired dish that you need to try out for yourself to believe how delicious it is. This is one tasty sushi dish that you will want to enjoy over and over again.

Yield: 6 Servings

Cooking Time: 1 Hour

List of Ingredients:

- 2 Cups of Rice, White in Color and Sushi Variety
- 2 Cups of Water
- 2 Tablespoons of Vinegar, Cider Variety
- 2 Chard Leaves, Fresh
- 2 Eggs, Large in Size and Beaten
- 2 Tablespoons of Soy Sauce, Evenly Divided
- 3 Tablespoons of Water
- 1 Onion, Finely Diced
- 1 tablespoon of Vegetable Oil
- ¾ Pound of Beef, Tenderloin Variety and Minced
- 1 can of Tuna, Light and Drained
- 1 Carrot, Fresh and Cut Julienne Style
- 6 Sheets of Seaweed, Dry

AAAAAAAAAAAAAAAAAAAAAAAAAAAAAAAAAAAAAAAAA

Instructions:

1. The first thing that you will want to do is make your rice. To do this bring your water and rice together in a medium sized saucepan. Bring to a boil. Then cover, reduce the heat and allow your rice to cook for at least 20 minutes or until your rice is tender and the water is fully absorbed. Remove from heat and season with your dash of your vinegar, stirring well to combine.

2. Then use a medium sized saucepan and boil your chard for at least a couple of minutes or until your chard is tender. Once tender cut into very thin strips.

3. Next whisk together your eggs, soy sauce and remaining water together until thoroughly combined. Pour this mixture into a hot skillet place over medium heat. Cook your mixture until thick in consistency. Once thick remove from heat and set aside to cool.

4. Then use a separate skillet and heat up some oil over medium to high heat. Once the oil is hot enough add in your onion and cook until it is tender. Once tender add in your minced beef and soy sauce and cook until your meat is browned evenly. Drain and set aside for later use.

5. Next place 1 sheet of your seaweed onto a bamboo mat. Then place a thin layer of rice onto your seaweed, making sure to leave some of the seaweed at the top uncovered.

6. Add all of your prepared ingredients on top of your rice, making sure to spread it evenly over the surface.

7. Wet the edges of your seaweed and begin to roll your sushi from the bottom tightly. Once rolled cut your roll into 4 equal sized pieces and repeat as necessary. Serve with some of your favorite soy sauce and strips of ginger and enjoy.

Recipe 14: Tasty Crawfish Sushi

If you haven't had the chance to try out crayfish for yourself, then you need to give this dish a try. Crayfish is packed full of healthy nutrients that your body needs. Once you get a bite I know you will begin to feel healthier.

Yield: 2 Servings

Cooking Time: 10 Minutes

List of Ingredients:

- 2 Cups of Potatoes, Boiled Variety
- 1 tablespoon of Oil, Mustard Variety
- 1 teaspoon of Vinegar, Rice Wine Variety
- 1 teaspoon of Mustard, Arranged Variety
- ½ teaspoons of Salt
- ½ teaspoons of Wasabi
- ½ Cup of Crawfish, Tails Only

AAAAAAAAAAAAAAAAAAAAAAAAAAAAAAAAAAAAAAAA

Instructions:

1. First combine all of your ingredients together except for your crawfish tails. Stir in a medium sized bowl until evenly combine.

2. Using a tablespoon, drop spoonfuls of your mixture onto a serving plate and top of with your crawfish tails. Serve with a small sized of soy sauce and enjoy whenever you are ready.

Recipe 15: Tasty Mango Roll

If you are looking for a sushi dish that will satisfy even your strongest sweet tooth, this is the perfect way to do it. This sushi dish is incredibly tasty and packed full of sweet flavor that I know you are going to want to make it over and over again.

Yield: 4 Servings

Cooking Time: 25 Minutes

List of Ingredients:

- 1 Egg, Large in Size and Beaten
- 1 Cup of Breadcrumbs, Panko Variety
- 12 Shrimps, Large in Size and Deveined
- ¼ Cup of Flour, All Purpose Variety
- Some Vegetable Oil, Deep Frying Only

Ingredients for Your Tartar Sauce:

- 2 Tablespoons of Onion, Minced
- 1 Egg, Boiled and Diced Finely
- 4 Tablespoons of Mayo
- 2 Tablespoons of Pickle, Minced
- Some Cabbage, Finely Shredded
- Dash of Salt for Taste
- Dash of Pepper for Taste

Ingredients for Your Roll:

- 1 Mango, Peeled and Diced
- 1 Avocado, Peeled and Diced
- Some Sesame Seeds, Black in Color and For Garnish
- ¼ Cup of Passion Fruit, Sauce Only
- 8 Ounces of Cream Cheese, Soft
- 2 Sheets of Seaweed, Dry
- 2 Cups of Rice, Sushi Variety

AAAAAAAAAAAAAAAAAAAAAAAAAAAAAAAAAAAAAAAAA

Instructions:

1. The first thing that you will want to do is coat your shrimp thoroughly in your all-purpose flour. Then dip it in your beaten egg and finally coat it in some bread crumbs. Once all of your shrimp has been coated place into a frying pan with your deep fr3ying oil and cook until your shrimp is evenly browned on all sides. Set on a plate lined with paper towels to drain.

2. While your shrimp is deep frying make your tartar sauce. To do this use a small sized bowl and combine all of your ingredients together until thoroughly combined.

3. Then prepare your mango rolls. To do this spread out your seaweed sheets onto a bamboo mat and top with your shrimp and tartar sauce right in the middle. Top with strips of your cream cheese and strips of your mango.

4. Wet the edges of your seaweed and begin to roll your sushi from the bottom tightly. Once rolled cut your roll into 10 equal sized pieces and repeat as necessary. Serve with some of your favorite soy sauce and strips of ginger and enjoy.

5. Garnish your roll with your black sesame seeds and drizzle your passion fruit juice over the top. Serve whenever you are ready.

Recipe 16: Hawaiian Style Sushi

If you are looking for a dish that will satisfy your taste buds, then this is the perfect sushi dish for you. Packed full of authentic Hawaiian sweet flavor, this is the perfect type of sushi for any person to thoroughly enjoy.

Yield: 4 Servings

Cooking Time: 20 Minutes

List of Ingredients:

- ½ Of an Avocado, Peeled and Cut into Thin Strips
- 7 Pieces of Crab, Imitation Variety and Cut into Thin Strips
- ½ teaspoons of Lemon, Fresh and Juice Only
- ½ A Cucumber, Fresh, Peeled and Cut into Thin Strips
- 2 Cups of Rice, Sushi Variety and Fully Cooked
- 1 Sheet of Seaweed, Dry
- 8 Pieces of Tuna, Cut Into Thin Strips

AAAAAAAAAAAAAAAAAAAAAAAAAAAAAAAAAAAAAAAAAA

Instructions:

1. Next place your seaweed onto a bamboo mat. Then place a thin layer of rice onto your seaweed.

2. Add your remaining ingredients on top of your rice and spread evenly throughout your rice. Press down lightly to press into the rice.

3. Wet the edges of your seaweed and begin to roll your sushi from the bottom tightly. Once rolled cut your roll into 6 to 8 equal sized pieces and repeat as necessary. Serve with some of your favorite soy sauce and strips of ginger and enjoy.

Recipe 17: Hearty Crab and Cream Cheese Sushi

Here is yet another easy sushi dish that I know you are going to love to make. Why spend a ton of money on this kind of sushi when you can make it from the comfort of your own home.

Yield: 2 Servings

Cooking Time: 1 Hour and 40 Minutes

List of Ingredients:

- 1 Cup of Rice, Sushi Variety and White in Color
- 2 Cups of Water
- 2 Tablespoons of Vinegar, Rice Variety
- 1 teaspoon of Salt, For Taste
- 2 Sheets of Seaweed, Dry
- ¼ of a Cucumber, Peeled and Sliced Finely
- 2 Pieces of Crab Legs, Imitation Variety
- ½ Pack of Cream Cheese, Soft and Sliced Finely
- 1 teaspoon of Ginger, Fresh and Minced

AAAAAAAAAAAAAAAAAAAAAAAAAAAAAAAAAAAAAAAA

Instructions:

1. The first thing that you will want to do is cook your rice. To do this bring both your rice and water together in a medium sized saucepan. Heat over high heat and once boiling reduce the heat to a simmer and allow your rice to cook until it is tender and the liquid has been fully absorbed. This should take about 20 minutes.

2. Stir in your vinegar and dash of salt, stirring well to evenly combine. Remove from heat and allow to cool for a couple of minutes.

3. Next place your seaweed onto a bamboo mat. Then place a thin layer of rice onto your seaweed.

4. Add your remaining ingredients on top of your rice and spread evenly throughout your rice. Press down lightly to press into the rice.

5. Wet the edges of your seaweed and begin to roll your sushi from the bottom tightly. Once rolled cut your roll into 5 to 6 equal sized pieces and repeat as necessary. Serve with some of your favorite soy sauce and strips of ginger and enjoy.

Recipe 18: Mexican Style Ceviche Roll

This is the perfect dish to make in the spring or summer time. Make the most out of your summer break by preparing this dish to enjoy on a terrace or in front of a fire pit. Either way I know you are going to like it.

Yield: 3 Servings

Cooking Time: 3 Hours and 20 Minutes

Ingredients for Your Ceviche:

- 6 Ounces of Snapper, Red Variety
- ¼ Cup of Lime Juice, Fresh
- 2 Tablespoons of Pineapple Juice, Fresh
- 2 Tablespoons of Orange Juice, Fresh
- 1 tablespoon of Bell Pepper, Yellow in Color and Diced Finely
- 1 tablespoon of Pepper, Serrano Variety and Diced Finely
- 1 tablespoon of Bell Pepper, Red in Color and Diced Finely
- 1 ½ Tablespoons of Onion, Red and Minced
- 2 Tablespoons of Cilantro, Fresh and Finely Chopped
- 1 teaspoon of Garlic, Minced
- ½ teaspoons of Salt for Taste
- 1 tablespoon of Olive Oil, Extra Virgin Variety

Ingredients for Your Roll:

- 3 Sheets of Seaweed, Dry
- 1 ½ Cups of Rice, Sushi Variety
- ½ A Grapefruit, Peeled and Cut into Segments
- ½ Of an Avocado, Large in Size, Pitted and Sliced Into thin Pieces
- ½ Tablespoons of Sesame Seeds, Black in Color
- Some Balsamic Vinegar, For Drizzling

AAAAAAAAAAAAAAAAAAAAAAAAAAAAAAAAAAAAAAAAAA

Instructions:

1. The first thing that you will want to do is make your ceviche. To do this use a shallow glass and add in all of your ingredients for your ceviche and toss thoroughly to coat.

2. Then cover and place into your fridge to chill for the next 3 hours, making sure to stir at least every hour or so. After this time remove from fridge and set aside.

3. Next make your sushi roll. To do this place your seaweed onto a bamboo mat. Then place a thin layer of rice onto your seaweed.

4. Add your remaining ingredients except for your sesame seeds and balsamic vinegar on top of your rice and spread evenly throughout your rice. Press down lightly to press into the rice.

5. Wet the edges of your seaweed and begin to roll your sushi from the bottom tightly. Once rolled cut your roll into 5 to 6 pieces and repeat as necessary. Serve with some of your favorite soy sauce and strips of ginger and enjoy. Garnish with your sesame seeds and drizzle your balsamic vinegar on top and serve whenever you are ready.

Recipe 19: Classic Michigan Style Roll

If you are looking for a sushi roll that packs quite a spicy punch, then this is one sushi dish that you have to try out for yourself. Packed full of spice yet incredibly delicious, this is one sushi dish that I know you won't be able to get enough of.

Yield: 2 Servings

Cooking Time: 15 Minutes

List of Ingredients:

- 6 Ounces of Tuna, Sashimi Variety

Ingredients for Your Spicy Filling:

- 1 Scallion, Finely Diced
- ½ Bell Pepper, Red in Color and Finely Diced
- ½ Avocado, Peeled and Finely Diced
- 1 ½ Cup of Rice, Sushi Variety
- Some Lime Juice, Fresh
- 2 Sheets of Seaweed, Dry
- Some Wasabi for Servings
- Some Mayo, Japanese Style
- Some Sriracha Sauce

AAAAAAAAAAAAAAAAAAAAAAAAAAAAAAAAAAAAAAA

Instructions:

1. The first thing that you will want to do is make your spicy filling. To do this combine your scallion, tuna, your Japanese mayo and Sriracha sauce. Stir thoroughly to evenly combine.

2. Then finely dice your bell pepper, avocado and fresh lime juice. Mix together until evenly combined.

3. Next place your seaweed onto a bamboo mat. Then place a thin layer of rice onto your seaweed.

4. Add your remaining ingredients on top of your rice and spread evenly throughout your rice. Press down lightly to press into the rice.

5. Wet the edges of your seaweed and begin to roll your sushi from the bottom tightly. Once rolled cut your roll into 8 equal sized pieces and repeat as necessary. Serve with some of your favorite soy sauce and strips of ginger and enjoy.

Recipe 20: Traditional Bacon Sushi Roll

Just as the name implies this is a traditional sushi dish for any who are looking to enjoy the authentic taste of Japanese cuisine. It is packed full of Japanese flavor and will soon become one of your favorite sushi dishes.

Yield: 8 Servings

Cooking Time: 1 Hour and 5 Minutes

List of Ingredients:

- 6 Sheets of Seaweed, Dry
- 3 Cups of Rice, White and Sushi Variety
- 6 Cups of Water
- 12 Pieces of Shrimp, Tempura Variety
- 1 Avocado, Peeled and Cut into Thin Strips
- 1 Onion, Green in Color and Cut into Thin Strips
- 6 Pieces of Bacon, Fully Cooked and Cut Into Thin Strips

AAAAAAAAAAAAAAAAAAAAAAAAAAAAAAAAAAAAAAAA

Instructions:

1. The first thing that you will want to do is cook your rice. To do this bring both your rice and water together in a medium sized saucepan. Heat over high heat and once boiling reduce the heat to a simmer and allow your rice to cook until it is tender and the liquid has been fully absorbed. This should take about 20 minutes.

2. Then prepare your shrimp. To do this cut off the tails and cut your shrimp lengthwise. Set aside for later use.

3. Next place your seaweed onto a bamboo mat. Then place a thin layer of rice onto your seaweed.

4. Add your remaining ingredients on top of your rice and spread evenly throughout your rice. Press down lightly to press into the rice.

5. Wet the edges of your seaweed and begin to roll your sushi from the bottom tightly. Once rolled cut your roll into 5 to 6 equal sized pieces and repeat as necessary. Serve with some of your favorite soy sauce and strips of ginger and enjoy.

Recipe 21: Vegetarian Style Sushi

This is a great tasting sushi dish that is great for any Vegetarian or Vegan. Feel free to use whatever kind of vegetables that you want to use. Just go with your preferred taste so you can make the ultimate sushi dish that you will love.

Yield: 4 Servings

Cooking Time: 1 Hour and 10 Minutes

List of Ingredients:

- 1 ½ Cups of Rice, White and Sushi Variety
- 1 ½ Cups of Water
- 1/3 Cup of Vinegar, Red Wine Variety
- 2 teaspoons of Water, Sugar
- 1 teaspoon of Salt
- ½ Avocado, Peeled and Sliced Finely
- 1 teaspoon of Lemon Juice, Fresh
- ¼ Cup of Sesame Seeds, As Needed
- ½ Cucumber, Peeled and Cut into Thin Sticks
- ½ Bell Pepper, Green in Color and Cut into Thin Sticks
- ½ Zucchini, Cut Into Thin Sticks

AAAAAAAAAAAAAAAAAAAAAAAAAAAAAAAAAAAAAAAA

Instructions:

1. The first thing that you will want to do is cook your rice. To do this bring both your rice and water together in a medium sized saucepan. Heat over high heat and once boiling reduce the heat to a simmer and allow your rice to cook until it is tender and the liquid has been fully absorbed. This should take about 20 minutes.

2. Then stir together your vinegar, white sugar and salt together in a small sized bowl. Stir thoroughly until the sugar fully dissolves. Pour this mixture into your rice and use a fork to thoroughly mix it together and to fluff your rice.

3. Then spread your rice onto a piece of parchment paper and cover with some paper towels that are damp. Allow your rice to cool.

4. Then place your avocado slices into a small sized bowl and drizzle with your fresh lemon juice.

5. Next place your seaweed onto a bamboo mat. Then place a thin layer of your sesame seeds onto your seaweed followed by a thin layer of your rice.

6. Add your remaining ingredients on top of your rice and spread evenly throughout your rice. Press down lightly to press into the rice.

7. Wet the edges of your seaweed and begin to roll your sushi from the bottom tightly. Once rolled cut your roll into 6 to 8 equal sized pieces and repeat as necessary. Serve with some of your favorite soy sauce and strips of ginger and enjoy.

Recipe 22: Philadelphia Sushi Roll

Here is yet another classic sushi dish for you and it is one that I know you are going to love. It is easy to make and packed full of flavor.

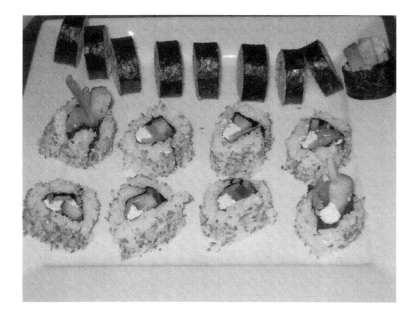

Yield: 4 Servings

Cooking Time: 30 Minutes

List of Ingredients:

- 8 Ounces of Cheddar, Cream Variety
- 3 Ounces of Salmon, Smoked Variety and Cut into Thin Strips
- 2 Cucumbers, Fresh and Cut Into Thin Strips
- 1 Onion, Green in Color and Cut into Thin Strips
- 2 Sheets of Seaweed, Dry
- 2 Cups of Rice, Sushi Variety and Fully Cooked

AAAAAAAAAAAAAAAAAAAAAAAAAAAAAAAAAAAAAAAAA

Instructions:

1. Place your seaweed onto a bamboo mat. Then place a thin layer of your fully cooked rice onto your seaweed.

2. Add your remaining ingredients on top of your rice and spread evenly throughout your rice. Press down lightly to press into the rice.

3. Wet the edges of your seaweed and begin to roll your sushi from the bottom tightly. Once rolled cut your roll into 5 to 6 equal sized pieces and repeat as necessary. Serve with some of your favorite soy sauce and strips of ginger and enjoy.

Recipe 23: Avocado and Brown Rice Sushi

If you are looking for a sushi dish that is a little more on the healthy side, then this is the dish you have been looking for. This is another great sushi recipe to make if you are new to sushi making. It is easy to make and tastes incredibly delicious.

Yield: 4 Servings

Cooking Time: 1 Hour and 15 Minutes

List of Ingredients:

- 1 Cup of Rice, White in Color and Sushi Variety
- 2 Cups of Water
- Dash of Sea Salt for Taste
- 1 tablespoon of Vinegar, Brown Rice Variety
- 1 Avocado, Peeled and Sliced Into Thin Sticks
- ¼ Of a Bell Pepper, Red in Color and Sliced Into Thin Sticks
- ¼ Cup of Alfalfa, Sprouts Only and For Taste
- 4 Sheets of Seaweed, Dry

AAAAAAAAAAAAAAAAAAAAAAAAAAAAAAAAAAAAAAA

Instructions:

1. The first thing that you will want to do is cook your rice. To do this firs thoroughly rinse your rice, then drain. Then bring both your rice, dash of sea salt and water together in a medium sized saucepan. Heat over high heat and once boiling reduce the heat to a simmer and allow your rice to cook until it is tender and the liquid has been fully absorbed. This should take about 20 minutes.

2. Next place your seaweed onto a bamboo mat. Then place a thin layer of rice onto your seaweed.

3. Add your remaining ingredients on top of your rice and spread evenly throughout your rice. Press down lightly to press into the rice.

4. Wet the edges of your seaweed and begin to roll your sushi from the bottom tightly. Once rolled cut your roll into 6 equal sized pieces and repeat as necessary. Serve with some of your favorite soy sauce and strips of ginger and enjoy.

Recipe 24: Buffalo Chicken Sushi

If you are looking for the perfect treat to make during this Sunday's football game, then this is the sushi recipe you need to try for yourself.

Yield: 4 Servings

Cooking Time: 25 Minutes

List of Ingredients:

- ½ Pound of Chicken Breasts, Fully Cooked and Chopped Finely
- ¼ Cup of Hot Sauce, Your Favorite Kind
- 4 Sheets of Seaweed, Dry
- 4 Cups of Rice, Sushi Variety and Fully Cooked
- 1 Carrot, Fresh, Peeled and Cut into Thin Strips
- 1 Stalk of Celery, Fresh and Cut into Thin Strips
- Some Spicy Mayo, Optional
- Some Fried Onions, Optional

AAAAAAAAAAAAAAAAAAAAAAAAAAAAAAAAAAAAAAAA

Instructions:

1. First mix together your chicken pieces and hot sauce together in a medium sized bowl until thoroughly combined.

2. Next place your seaweed onto a bamboo mat. Then place a thin layer of rice onto your seaweed.

3. Add your remaining ingredients on top of your rice and spread evenly throughout your rice. Press down lightly to press into the rice.

4. Wet the edges of your seaweed and begin to roll your sushi from the bottom tightly. Once rolled cut your roll into 8 equal sized pieces and repeat as necessary. Serve with some of your favorite soy sauce and strips of ginger and enjoy.

Recipe 25: Healthy Quinoa and Brown Rice Sushi

Here is yet another healthy sushi recipe that you are going to love if you are looking to make the healthiest type of sushi possible. This dish is packed full of helpful protein and is one of the lightest sushi recipes you will find.

Yield: 4 Servings

Cooking Time: 1 Hour and 25 Minutes

List of Ingredients:

- 2/3 Cup of Rice, Brown Variety
- 2 1/3 Cups of Water
- Dash of Sea Salt, For Taste
- 2 Tablespoons of Vinegar, Rice Variety
- 1 tablespoon of Vinegar, Cider Variety
- 1 tablespoon of Mirin, Optional
- 2 Tablespoons of Sugar, Turbinado Variety
- ½ teaspoons of Sea Salt, For Taste
- ½ Cup of Quinoa, Uncooked
- 4 Sheets of Seaweed, Dry
- ½ A Carrot, Shredded Finely
- ½ A Cucumber, Cut Into Thin Sticks
- 1 Avocado, Peeled and Cut into Thin Sticks

AAAAAAAAAAAAAAAAAAAAAAAAAAAAAAAAAAAAAAAAA

Instructions:

1. The first thing that you will want to do is cook your brown rice. To do this bring both your brown rice, dash of sea salt and water together in a medium sized saucepan. Heat over high heat and once boiling reduce the heat to a simmer and allow your rice to cook for about 20 to 30 minutes.

2. Then use a medium sized bowl and add in both of your vinegars, sea salt, white sugar and mirin together. Whisk thoroughly until your sugar fully dissolves.

3. Next add your quinoa into your rice and stir thoroughly to combine. Bring this mixture to a boil and then reduce the heat to a simmer. Cook your rice and quinoa together until both are tender and your liquid has fully absorbed. This should take about 15 minutes.

4. Once down move your rice and quinoa mixture into a separate bowl and mix in your vinegar mixture. Stir thoroughly to combine. Allow your mixture to cool until it is slightly warm, making sure to stir it occasionally.

5. Next place your seaweed onto a bamboo mat. Then place a thin layer of rice onto your seaweed.

6. Add your remaining ingredients on top of your rice and spread evenly throughout your rice. Press down lightly to press into the rice.

7. Wet the edges of your seaweed and begin to roll your sushi from the bottom tightly. Once rolled cut your roll into 5 to 6 equal sized pieces and repeat as necessary. Serve with some of your favorite soy sauce and strips of ginger and enjoy.

About the Author

Molly Mills always knew she wanted to feed people delicious food for a living. Being the oldest child with three younger brothers, Molly learned to prepare meals at an early age to help out her busy parents. She just seemed to know what spice went with which meat and how to make sauces that would dress up the blandest of pastas. Her creativity in the kitchen was a blessing to a family where money was tight and making new meals every day was a challenge.

Molly was also a gifted athlete as well as chef and secured a Lacrosse scholarship to Syracuse University. This was a blessing to her family as she was the first to go to college and at little cost to her parents. She took full advantage of her college education and earned a business degree. When she graduated, she joined her culinary skills and business acumen into a successful catering business. She wrote her first e-book after a customer asked if she could pay for several of her recipes. This sparked the entrepreneurial spirit in Mills and she thought if one person wanted them, then why not share the recipes with the world!

Molly lives near her family's home with her husband and three children and still cooks for her family every chance she gets. She plays Lacrosse with a local team made up of her old teammates from college and there are always some tasty nibbles on the ready after each game.

Don't Miss Out!

Scan the QR-Code below and you can sign up to receive emails whenever Molly Mills publishes a new book. There's no charge and no obligation.

Sign Me Up

https://molly.gr8.com